BACKUP 2.0

RECO-WORRY TO RECOVERY,

One Habit is Enough

One Habit is Enough

KAMAL GULATI

Worldwide Published by
Pendown Press

PENDOWN PRESS

An ISO 9001 & ISO 14001 Certified Co.,

Regd. Office: 2525/193, 1st Floor, Onkar Nagar-A,

Tri Nagar, Delhi-110035

Ph.: 09350849407, 09312235086

E-mail: info@pendownpress.com

Branch Office: 1A/2A, 20, Hari Sadan, Ansari Road,

Daryaganj, New Delhi-110002

Ph.: 011-45794768

Website: PendownPress.com

First Edition: 2023

ISBN: 978-93-5554-535-0

Layout and Cover Designed by Pendown Graphics Team

Illustration Designed by Pendown Illustration Team

Printed and Bound in India by Thomson Press India Ltd.

You are a Real Hero doing Real Work. Real Breakdowns are bound to happen with Computer Data Availability & Family.

Here is presenting Mr. Backup 2.0 beyond your current & default Backup 1.0 to get you Back Up under all circumstances to cover your back for both Data & Family.

Your Organisation & Family Will grow to extent you are Ready for Getting Back UP in case of Real Breakdowns.

Contents

Foreword 1

Acknowledgement 5

Story: "Reco-worry to Recovery,
Mr. Backup 2.0: One Habit is Enough" 9

1. Introduction 15

A. About Me 16

B. Who is This Book For? 17

C. Story of Our Organization 18

D. Story: Why this book? 24

E. Some Hard Facts which could Impact Reputation and Business 30

2. The 9 Transformational Habits 32

Family 2.0	Habit	Backup 2.0
1. The Mindset of Family is one of the top 2 always.	Mindset	The Mindset of Backup/Data Criticality Top 3
2. Think & Involve those who bring in Love & Care: Spouse, Children & Elders.	Involvement	Think & Involve those who bring in Money: Business people
3. (3) Generations being taken care of by couple (2) Raising children together as (1) Treating both sides of the Family as (1) (0) issues of love lost	3-2-1-1-0	3 copies of the Data 2 types of medium 1 offsite 1 offline or cloud & immutable 0 errors on Backup

4. Relevance of Old Customs/ Material/Assets.	Relevance	Only Relevant Data to be Backed Up
5. Why are Extended Family & Friends Critical?	Extensions	Question why is some data not Backed Up?
6. Bring in Money Aspects as well.	Monetization	Think Monetization of Data
7. Measure Love & Care	Management of unstructured	Structure for Unstructured Data
8. Rule Book for all in Family democratically with a dash of authority	Rule Book	Business Continuity Plan from Backup side Rule Book.
9. Future Plan including Visioning, Planning, Skilling, Safety net, Education, Insurance, Will Writing	Future	Future Direction for Data Backup

3. How Come One Habit is Enough? 74

4. Going The Extra Mile: Sustainability/ESG, Business Continuity Plan/Resilience & Backup 80

5. Case Studies: Mirrors Reflecting The Truth 90

- Case Study 1
- Case Study 2

6. Backup Vs Back Up, The Evolution of Backup & Related Storage: Fun Facts 96

7. Conclusion 102

Foreword

"Don't judge me by my Success, Judge me by how many times I fall and get back up."

~Nelson Mandela

I feel privileged to be writing the foreword for this unique IT book written in the form of a story that comes across as a breath of fresh air.

The author Kamal Gulati's evolution brings me great happiness, and I am comforted by the thought that he will keep evolving as long as he is alive to make a bigger and bigger impact on each organization and individual he comes in contact with. He is a man on a mission now. Since this book is in the form of a conversational story, I am writing the foreword, too, as actual conversations between Kamal and me.

12th Dec 2011, 11.00 AM

Me: "Kamal, I got this mail 30 mins back about the ASG takeover of Atempo and restructuring in India. What is it?

Kamal, on the other side: "The India team exists for 30 days only. I am still digesting it, but thanks for reaching out in these testing times".

I say: "Let us meet tomorrow right in the morning at 9.15 AM; we've jointly got multiple great customers to take care of whom we onboarded in the last couple of years."

13th Dec 2011, 9. 45 AM

Me: "Kamal, how come you are late for the 1st time for our meeting? You look exhausted, just relax; it will all work out. What do you want- a job for you and anyone in your team is not an issue, but I am a little concerned about you.

Kamal: "Tarunjee, I am just thinking hard with my team and wife. I am not concerned about finding a job; our promises to our customers and taking care of their interests is the major issue on hand".

Me: "Be specific about what is in your mind?"

Kamal: "Could we create an organization to take care of all these customers? I am not sure how this would work out and if I can even handle it on my own".

I cannot believe what I am hearing, I say: "A young man wanting to start his entrepreneurial journey doubting his capabilities even though demonstrating such calm and courage in the face of such a breakdown, it is rare for any country manager to think like this. I am delighted. I will work with you in creating structures for you to succeed in your entrepreneurial journey. I, too, started with little money and no background."

Thus began a new organization led by a tentative yet bold young man and his loyal team. Even the Global Outgoing Atempo team supported them remarkably during the tough transition phase, which was hard for them as well.

Fast forward to June 2021, Kamal had just lost his mom and a few critical employees during the peak covid period.

On the condolence call, he asked me: "What are you up to, Tarunjee?

I said: "A great 2nd innings to support organizations with funds, *tu apni suna* [How's it going for you?]

I see lots of small organizations closing shop or restructuring totally." I poked him such that he opened up.

Kamal: "Tarunjee, my mission is clear. These 6 months have been tough as I could not focus as much as I wanted to, but now we should ensure that the Backup Industry grows phenomenally. I will keep reaching out to veterans like you for input; the Josh [Enthusiasm] is high. Mom is gone physically, and I have a few breakdowns to handle in the Family, but I am clear that contributing to the growth of my Industry is the way to celebrate her life and the values that she gave me."

This is Kamal & his organization itSimple, from a tentative start to an Organization on a Mission for this critical, under-valued IT Backup and Archival Industry- Working toward making a Backup Mindset prevalent in all corporate people.

As of now, it is not a question of "IF" but "When" & "How Many Breakdowns/Ransomware Attacks."

I am told 85% of organizations faced Ransomware attacks last year, and multiple other breakdowns of different kinds happened in the last 3 years of the Covid period.

I am sure you will love the narrative of this book, which would contribute to your personal and professional skills in a simple yet effective manner. Things are always simple; it is only our thinking that makes it complicated.

By Mr. Tarun Seth, A visionary, Always Positive against all odds. Ex - MD Hitachi Systems micro clinic Ltd. Now Running Aton Capital Pvt Ltd.

Acknowledgement

I want to thank each reader, starting with you, for taking time out to read this niche book for taking care of your critical computer data, which has been referred to as New OIL by Clive Humby in 2006. Later our very own Mukesh Ambani reiterated this in 2019 and started investing big money to get more data for each one us (Indians). Your devoting time to read this book shows the kind of openness you have for learning something new, in a line that you have possibly been part of, for some considerable time.

You and your work are the "Real Hero" working on IT data, its Backup, BCP & Sustainability for your organization and our work is like a background to your main work.

That is how we wish to remain, we are covering your back, with the our consistent efforts to serve you at next plateaus, and this book, "Mr. Backup 2.0." is a part of our efforts to make you completely equipped to excel and become an even "Bigger Hero."

Acknowledging Sanjay Dutta, my senior colleague. He has spent 28+ years in the Storage, Backup field as a part of multiple MNCs and, as an entrepreneur for the last 10 years, has made a significant contribution in the writing of this book.

Daman Dev Sood, My senior in TCS days, who has spent decades in BCP, and now in Sustainability, has contributed largely to the section on BCP/Sustainability. Heartful Acknowledgement for him.

Humble Thanks to our current and ex-team members, including but not limited to Achin Manocha, Manoj Dawra, Sachin Srivastava, Avinash Pandey, Rajeev Mishra, Arvind Chauhan, Sanjay Joshi, Pallavi Chauhan, Shristi Mittal, Richa Batra, Sonia, Rajeev Ranjan, Syed Rizwan, Punit Saxena, Sudhanshu Sharma, CL Gupta, Gaurav Bajpai, Rohit, Lave, Aditya & Kush Tyagi, Sachin Kumar, Sudhir Sharma, Ankur, and Saurabh Narula. Saurabh, Arvind and Manoj gave key inputs for this book.

I also wish to thank each one of my Lakhs of past (Atempo, IBM, TCS, and Elnova times) and present customers & channel partners. Pains, challenges, long discussions and the pathway of each one of these made me learn something new, which made it possible for me, to come up with the solutions that are presented here in this book.

My heartfelt thanks to some of my special ex-colleagues & bosses in all the organizations I worked for, including but not limited to Jon Foster, Neal Ater, Gurprit Gulati, NGS, Sanjiv Tandon, Kevyn Ho, Paul Walman, V Subra, Kaushik Bagchi, Tapan Mehta, Anil Mennon, Piyush Rakhecha, Devesh Gupta, Seema Mehra, Arun Singhal, Gurpreet Singh, Dr Sanjay Goel, Binny Jhamb, Vijay K Mehra, Sanjay Duggal, Yogesh Lakhani, Venkata Ramani, Bharti Munjal, Vijay Vohra, Vikas Agarwal, Jatin Bajaj, Neeta Sambre, Venkat, Tushar Gupta and Kapil Kocher.

Immense gratitude towards my mentors and coaches, who never gave up on me despite the silly mistakes I made. This includes Akshar Yadav (my inspiration for writing this book which I have been thinking for a while but he made me complete this), Gurmeet Singh Khurana, Mahesh Nambiar, Gurprit Gulati, Ferdi D'souza, Hiren Modi, Vivek Chopra, Praveen Puri, Gopal Rao, Balvinder Singh Sodhi, Vikas Goel, Krishna Kumar, Parminder Singh Nagi, Prabha, Nirav Vyas, Nasreen Khan, Lalit Khorana, Arun Kumar, Dipanshu Vijay, Mohit Wadhawan, Chetan Jain, Naveen Banura, Vipil Gupta to name a few.

Special thanks to my RECW classmates who keep inspiring me to study more (possibly to compensate for the less studies that I did in college ☺), some of them being Buddha Neeraj Pathu, Atul Lotiya Pathan, Vivek Mahesh Babu, Ghanshu Shushil Gupta, Narendra Kureel Anna, Chinna Praveen Verma, Khujju Vikas Garg, Uchakta Ashish Agarwal, Shatru Singh, Bhattoo Ritu Raj, Gau Gaurav Gupta, Sanjay Gullu, Panditg Sanjay Thripathi, Rohit Mukerjee (Bengali Babu), Bhushan Pati, Gupta Brothers (Prateek & Ashish), SP Srivastava , Aloo Alok Srivastava, Manoj Vachani Bund, Tokhi Santokh Singh, Chikna Javed, Anil Tyagi, Sunil Balan. Sunil balan, Shatru & Hari P gave me decent inputs for this book.

My dear extended family members and close friends, also need to be mentioned here, acknowledgements for loving me, and my naughty Karmas [Deeds] (my apologies, if I miss out any one), Grovers, Sachdevas, Khandpurs, Vizs, Chawlas, Gulatis of Delhi & Ludhiana, Tandon Uncle, Sudhesh Aunty,

Narulas, Madhoks, Bile Chacha, Pramod Singh, Akhil Goel, Narendra Kamra, Sandeep Manchanda, Ruchi Bambri, Nishi, Atul Kapur, Atul Modi, Sanjay Agarwal, Gurprit Gulati, Sandeep/Sunaina Khanna, Anil Gupta, Nitin Aggarwal, Hemant, Ashok Kumar, Vishal Bindra and Somesh Rastogi. Rajeev Mamidanna need special mention for key inputs.

Last but not least, biggest thanks to my immediate family, Parents (Santosh Maa, Satya Prakash Papa) & Parents in Law (Avinash Maa, Ram Paul Grover Papa), soulmate Ruchi, Children Saksham & Tavishi, big sister Simi, sisters (Surbhi, Suman, Madhavi, Saanchie), Jijus (Rakesh, Vinay, Ajay, Munish, Madhu), Usha Maa, Choti Sasu Maa, Rajiv Bhai, Tina Bhabhi, Simi Madhok, and Tushar, Sankalp, Eshita, Ritika, Varun & Big Saishu.

I am thankful to My Friend Dinesh Verma, CEO, Pendown Press and his team for their support and suggestions throughout the creative process.

Story: Reco-worry to Recovery, Mr. Backup 2.0: One Habit is Enough

Who among us doesn't love a good story? Everyone does!

So, let's start our conversation with a very interesting story that I am sure all of you will relate to.

Once upon a time, there lived a young yet wise and experienced Data Guru named Aankade. Aankade had dedicated his young life to taking care of the critical data of the people in his Kingdom. The Kingdom he lived in was digitally empowered and thrived on advanced technology, a paperless E-Kingdom that took great pride in being the most modern and prosperous Kingdom in the entire region.

Aankade had made it his life mission to make people aware consistently that data loss could be catastrophic, causing people to lose their memories, their health, their work, their defense, their future and their livelihoods, and he kept working toward this consistently. He talked with all the influencers and decision-makers in the King's Court, Finance, Defense, Interior, and Commerce Ministries.

He always talked about & worked for precious data Backup and tried to make people aware of why they should not take it for granted. He was committed to creating a mindset shift among all stakeholders responsible for data.

Initially, they were all reluctant, but he refused to give up even in the face of taunts and ridicule. They would all call him mad and eccentric behind his back and even to his face sometimes.

They kept telling him; you are delusional. Why should we waste so much money on something that brings no returns and does not even impact the working and living of the Kingdom? We would rather spend that much money on new research and development to create even better and faster technology.

However, he kept persisting in multiple different ways by giving them examples of other kingdoms who had neglected Backup as they were doing and had lost everything when taken unaware by malware and ransomware attacks.

Finally, with great effort and perseverance, he was able to convince a core group of the Kingdom's decision-makers. He got them enrolled in data Backup criticality, & got a budget approved for the same.

However, there was one condition, they asked that this mission be secret, as they did not want to seem like fools for having taken the wrong decision in case Data Backup didn't prove to be useful.

Aankade agreed and put together a special team that began Mission Backup 2.0 secretly and silently in all the core areas of operation of the entire Kingdom. He created a "Data Backup Rule Book" for how data could be backed up and retrieved within 2 hrs to 24 hrs. This would ensure Medical, Educational,

Commerce and Defense, all critical infra would be up and running under all circumstances with zero downtime.

He also ensured the implementation of a Data Backup Rule Book so that everybody involved would be in sync and there would be clear SOPs for all to follow.

Following the 3-2-1-1-0 Backup rule, ensuring that they had three copies of the data, on two different mediums, with one offsite & one on cloud, he made sure to meet the requirements of different ministry departments through **Dry Runs** for the authenticity of data within requisite RPO/RTO.

He also utilized cloud backup with intelligence, helping the Kingdom optimize data storage and reduce storage costs. As a result, they were able to create a secure and efficient Backup strategy to protect their data from any disaster.

One night, a terrible storm hit the Kingdom. Everybody was worried that the storm could cause widespread damage and lead to serious data loss. They all, including the King, thought that everything would be lost as the storm had destroyed almost everything. They expected life to come to a standstill and for the Kingdom to lose its prosperity.

The king and the common man were all scared that they would have to build their Kingdom and their lives from scratch once again. It would be a tedious, tough and long process.

But Aankade was cool & confident that he and his team had worked diligently to protect data and for it to be available under all eventualities & all would be well.

The core group of decision-makers who had invested in Aankade's Backup plan were waiting with bated breath to see whether they had made the right decision.

As the storm abated and morning broke, the assessment of damages began- the Kingdom was badly affected, and many people lost their homes and possessions. But Aankade's Backup strategy proved to be a saving grace.

Aankade and his team went to work to restore the lost data, ensuring that everyone had their memories, their health records, their work, their Kingdom's Defense, their future and their livelihoods. Defense & Health was hit only 10%, as 90% could work from alternate infra available to them & even the balance 10% was up and running within 2 hrs.

The Kingdom was able to get back on its feet in very little time with minimal losses. Everyone within the Kingdom and in the surrounding regions was amazed.

Aankade, when asked how he could achieve such a fantastic achievement for his Kingdom, said, "A Backup Mindset for sure!"

"Each one of us, in our own ways, does Backup our phone data, physical & digital assets, and computers, but do we do it methodically?"

"Remember to audit the Backup for workability and time in which it would work from RPO/RTO perspective under various failure scenarios, calling this **"Backup 2.0"** he further went on to add, "There could be two habits which are most critical, one Rule Book for Business continuity from a Backup perspective and second questioning consistently whether I have the Mindset of data & its Backup being critical. If you have this Mindset, the rest of the habits come naturally, ensuring that you have a system for current and future data Backup requirements."

Over time, Aankade became famous in the land for his work as **"Mr. Backup 2.0"**. His Kingdom prospered as people knew their data was safe and secure. Aankade's team continued to ensure that the Backup systems were always up to date, and the people of the Kingdom knew that their data was in good hands.

As time went on, other kingdoms heard about Aankade's backup strategy and began to adopt similar practices. The people in these kingdoms also came to realize the importance of data Backup and how it could save them from all kinds of disasters.

In the end, Aankade's legacy lived on as the "Mr Backup 2.0" who had protected the data of his Kingdom and taught others the importance of Backup. His story inspired many to take the necessary steps to protect their own data and preserve it for the future.

This story of Annakade's Kingdom gets played out in different ways for every single organization and largely for every individual having any kind of data but in view of day-to-day operational aspects, regular working of organization & individual life.

Life & organization are not impacted by Backup directly; the major importance becomes, Cyber security, cloud, ERP,

CRM, and other operations applications. And as Backup does not have any utility apart from recovery in case of Disaster, it gets "taken for granted", especially for

- Small to mid-size organizations or
- Even specific segments of even large organizations

Either they don't have well-detailed processes and policies, or these processes and policies are not followed well and revised well from time to time.

- In these interesting times, it is critical to look at how your critical data will be available to you despite whatever crisis. These are interesting times, given that Data is a matter of business differentiation as well as survival.
- Cyber attacks, issues such as Ransomware attacks, are on the rise and are seen the most in our beloved country.
- Insider threats, Job switches, and Organizational loyalty are not at the same level where they used to be.
- Increased complexity leads to human, software & infra glitches.

> **All these are part of the Backup 2.0**
>
> Mindset is one Critical Habit for any major Result that one wishes to cause beyond the Ordinary.

1

INTRODUCTION

A. About Me
B. Who is this book for?
C. The Story of Our Organization
D. Why this book? The Story!
E. Some Hard Facts which could Impact Reputation and Business

1A.
About Me

Hi, I am an entrepreneur running ITS Technology Solution Pvt. Ltd (Brand Name "itSimple"), India's 1st organization which is 100% focused on Software Data Backup and Archival, and provide Emergency support 24X7.

We have served the best of the names in Indian Corporate & Government verticals and 20 different countries. Organizations have been trusting us for over 10 years consistently.

The journey of dreaming of running my own business started right from NIT Warangal times in the early 90s. It was triggered by seeing my father struggle to make a few thousand rupees in his mechanical workshop and yet talk about his vision- our vision of setting up a reasonably sized organization to serve humanity with passion and intent.

Hearing him talk about this vision motivated me to participate actively in the entrepreneurship development cell and different communication clubs and finally join a niche Power Backup organization Elnova, despite offers from big companies like HCL. Then the rich corporate world job experience went on for nearly 20 years with TCS, IBM, Atempo SA in various responsible positions in related software products field.

1B.
Who is this book for?

This book will be extremely useful for Anyone and Everyone who considers Computer Data to be important for whatever reasons. However, this book will prove transformational specifically for:

- CIO or IT Professional of a mid-size organization
- Business owner of a Small & Medium Enterprise
- IT Professional or Consultant, or
- Anybody who aspires to be one of the above

1C.

The Story of Our Organization

9.30 AM 12th Dec 2011

I entered the office whistling; I was high on the success of our biggest win of the year. "Good morning, team. What is special on this winter morning?" I asked my team jovially. Just then, our IP phone rang Tring Tring Tring…

"Hi Kamal, could you get the whole team on speaker phone? I have an important message to convey". The management calling this late at night from the USA was surprising, to say the least.

"Team, Atempo has been taken over by ASG, 20 times its size, good for the product, but you guys in India have only 30 days!

Write to me if any one of you wishes to ask something, and if appropriate, it will be replied to. India is special; hence we are calling personally."

Hearing this, I go numb. It is near impossible to process this shocking announcement out of the blue. I tell the team, "Give me a few minutes".

My whole professional world had come crashing down, the efforts of the last 3 years, building the brand from scratch, investing even my salary into growing the organization's business. What was happening was unbelievable. I had never seen this coming. However, the team is outside waiting for me. I take a deep breath to center myself and go out to interact with the team.

I walk in confidently, exuding a calm I definitely do not feel inside, and I say to the team, "Team, let us sit in the conference room and figure out our next steps."

Sonu, *sab ke liye badhiya* coffee *banao,* and get special Hot Aloo Chaat. [I ask the pantry attendant to make coffee and get comforting warm snacks for everyone].

Further, I say, "Manoj/Rizwan order something for yourselves in Mumbai/Banglore, please."

The moment I stop speaking, I am surrounded by a panicked babble of voices. It feels as if I am listening from somewhere far away.

Employee 1: *"Boss naukari to lagwa doge naa?"* [Boss, you'll help us find a job, I hope!]

Employee 2: "Customer *ko kya jawaab denge, abhi toh* complex case *ka* payment collect *kiya hai."* [How will we answer the customers? I have just picked up the payment for a complex case.]

Employee 3: "*Hum sab Saath hain kuch to sochenge sab ke liye*" [We are all in this together, we'll find a way]

Employee 4: "Let us check our mail; there might be details.

Arre, yeh toh mail has gone to all customers/partners about restructuring in multiple organizations, including India. It says a possible new ASG team and a strong ASG mean a bright future for the product."

This is like another bomb on an unsuspecting target. I need some time to process this. Again I say to the team. "Team give me a few minutes with myself."

And then the dam broke loose- Customers/partners started reaching out to us.

"*Kamal kya soch raha hai, mai tera poora saath dunga*, you have a strong team." [Kamal, what are you thinking? I will support you completely. You have a strong team.]

"Kya ho raha hai bhai, tere ko naukari chahiiye kya" [What is happening brother, Do you need a Job.]

"Kamal, relax and think hard. Let us meet up tomorrow."

Jitne mu utni baate, many people offer opinions and advice.

The scene shifts to my Home

I narrated the whole shocking episode to my wife, Ruchi. After hearing me out without interruption, she reached out to hold my hand gently but firmly, and this is what she had to say: "Trust yourself, whatever you are thinking, I know you can make it work. I am there with you no matter what you choose".

After dinner, I went into the study and sat quietly pondering over the situation for quite some time. The faces of my team kept haunting me, the hope and confidence in their eyes that I would find a way out, their firm belief in my capabilities, Ruchi's unconditional faith and support and my own desire to always impact the world positively- all this motivated me to find a unique solution to the unpleasant and unpredictable situation.

I took stock of what I had going for me and how I could leverage it to build even more- 50+ leading customer sites, an annuity of 40 Lakh Rupees, 8 champion employees, a monthly outflow of 7 Lakhs- and then I came to a momentous decision.

What had seemed like the biggest blow of my life now looked like a gift- the biggest opportunity of my life to date.

It was the perfect opportunity and time to join the tribe of entrepreneurs creating "Financial Abundance for Self & others while contributing significantly to the country's economy."

My mind was made up; I would not let this opportunity pass by. I called the OEM Management and made this life-altering statement, "I wish to take over Atempo India and convert it into an independent unit. What support can you get me?"

The reply was heartening and encouraging. "That's great, though unexpected, we are delighted. It will be challenging, but let us see how to work this out."

Hats off to Atempo, WOW! Not many global OEMs would do it; unbelievable. More so in a tough transition phase. However, when the intention is to serve customers and take care of employees, great companies do whatever it takes.

Atempo India became "ITS Technology Solution Private Limited"; itSimple in its present form, came into existence on 1st Sep 2012. itSimple Stands for "it is Simple", which means:

"Backup is Simple" is stated in Hindi as "Backup Saral Hai."

We have never looked back since that momentous day!

itSimple is known for being sustainable, "caring & doing whatever it takes 100%, itSimple", under all circumstances.

We retained each & every employee & customer; a few of them even worked 10+ years post that unforgettable event, and we are serving 90% of those customers even to date.

1D.
Why This Book? The Story!

"Once upon a time (haha, obviously not that long ago, but any story worth telling needs to begin with once upon a time ☺), there was an IT professional, Ashutosh Mehra. His father earned just enough to take care of day-to-day expenses.

Though things were difficult financially, it was a blessing that Ashutosh was a bright scholar and made it to a Decent Government Engineering College. Though he studied Mechanical Engineering, he always had a fascination for Computers. In his free time, he started his orientation towards computers, much beyond what his curriculum taught him.

When a person is determined, the universe also supports them in every manner bringing them the right guides and opportunities. This happened with Ashutosh too. He found a mentor who worked in a good organization and, thus, thankfully, a Job in the IT department as a fresher.

Taking care of his parents and sisters and being able to afford the expenses of his sister's marriages was Ashutosh's driving force when he began working. He wanted to prove himself and earn well, so he typically worked 14 hrs a day.

This 14-hour work day continued like this despite a change of a couple of Jobs. In fact, as he grew in his career, his work day only got extended in the next 20 years.

Ashutosh is now a part of the top management of a reputed organization; he has built a beautiful home, got married and has a wonderful wife and 2 lovely children.

Today his entire Family, including his parents, can afford all the luxuries of life.

One day like any other sitting in an office workshop about where they are headed in life, Ashutosh is confronted with a shocking truth!

The initial exercises made him open up and see deeper. This is what Ashutosh had to say "I hardly take care of spending time with my wife, children, both sets of parents, sisters and their families. I take them for granted. They are the reason I started working long hours, and I wanted to provide for them well and now, even after we have so much, I am still slogging 14hrs a day at the office."

There was stunned silence. What was a boring workshop suddenly became a hub of activity, with everyone telling each other that this was happening in their life too. Everyone's eyes were opened to a not-so-pleasant but undeniable truth.

The instructor told Ashutosh, "Wow, you are seeing something new; that is an amazing insight."

The instructor began working with Ashutosh in-depth, and the picture that came up was eye-opening, to say the least.

This is what Ashutosh's family life looked like:

Lesser and lesser time with Family, bare minimum need-based communication, minimal knowledge of what the Family was going through, teenage children becoming more screen-centric, generation gap arising between parents & children, possibly the last few years left with parent's life and the children staying at Home.

All this was making him lonely and disconnected from the Family. As a result, he was deeply unhappy despite doing well at work. Whatever is said and done, our Family is our backbone and is critical to our joy and peace of mind.

The instructor then worked with him to set up further sessions to get him to create a new future of FUN & CONNECTION with his FAMILY in detail with multiple new actions and habits.

Then the instructor asked him to take a look at which similar aspect of the Office Ashutosh was taking for granted. Taken aback by the Question, Ashutosh pondered over it for a bit. Then he replied without hesitation- "IT Data & its Backup, which is absolutely critical, yet keeps being put on the back burner. I, as the overall infra head earlier, had bought one tool, but now the Backup Subject Matter Expert, P Venkat, keeps asking for further aspects to be covered beyond the standard Backup tool for automated Backup; I stop him saying there are more pressing needs for operational software, cloud and cyber security."

"He keeps telling me that the organization is not ready for a Data Disaster and his job and the organization's data are at great risk."

"Venkat even gave me an example of a Ransomware attack on a neighbouring organization of a similar size, resulting in a 7-day production shutdown, leading to a whopping 40+ Cr loss., and even a few IT persons losing their jobs, but I just keep telling him to relax. I keep assuring him that I have seen these aspects enough. We have much, much better IT Security tools and a much more responsible IT team than that organization."

"However, seeing this in the light of how I am ignoring my Family and taking them for granted, I now realize that I am making the same mistake with the IT Backup at work."

"Both Family & Data Backup are critical for a person's success and security. Yet, they are so subtle that we take them for granted, undermining their importance until a disaster strikes."

"I understand Venkat is under constant stress and possibly even looking for a safer Job.

This workshop has truly opened my eyes to what I am in danger of losing. That which is perhaps most important in my life, or for that matter, in every person's life."

"I will ensure that we go in for an extensive assessment of what further can be done for every aspect of Data Backup, such as where the Backup stands and what further is required, and what the future holds."

Then it struck Ashutosh that Backup is like INSURANCE, required yet largely ignored; we get to know of its seriousness only when disaster strikes, then we remember it for some time after that, and it is forgotten again.

In life, we cannot possibly practice Drills for Disaster, but in the Corporate world, this is certainly possible. And now that he had become aware, Ashutosh decided to take immediate action.

He invited his Infra Head Mrs. Sunita Reddy & Backup Subject Matter Expert, Mr. P Venkat, for a detailed interaction to create and set into motion multiple habits and processes organization-wide for complete and continuous Backup.

He took action on the home front, too; he made time to talk with both sides of parents, his wife Sadhavi & children Sambhav and Aanvi, to understand what they expected of him, what made them happy, what they enjoyed doing, and then align his actions to provide them with the care/love and time they deserved., He committed himself to creating detailed habits for both his organizational data Backup & Care/Love for his Family, his true Backup system in life.

BACKUP 2.0

His team came up with an interesting suggestion. They said, "Let us call our new commitment and practices of Backup as (Backup 2.0) and stick to it religiously as the default way of doing things, (Backup 1.0) did not work for us, leaving us with a lot of Reconciliation Worry (Reco…Worry)."

Venkat Said "We are clear that this Backup 2.0 will mark a new beginning for our organization creating data being available under all circumstances and evolving this consistently over a period, and PEACE OF MIND & fulfilment to me as well."

Taking a cue from his team's suggestion, Ashutosh said

Family 2.0

"How about we all decide to create a similar habit system for Happiness in our Family (our Life Backup) to replace the worry and guilt that we currently battle with and call this habit system as Family 2.0."

"We would all create habits for both Backup 2.0 & Family 2.0, I want each one of us to have happiness in our respective individual families, and as one large organizational family, we should even plan Family outings in different official teams for bonding & contribution."

1E.
Some Hard Facts which could Impact Reputation and Business

Since the beginning of this book, I have been talking about how important Backup is, but as you all know, talking alone is never enough. One needs to walk that talk too.

So here are some hard facts, that will leave you in no doubt about the critical importance of Backup.

- 80% of SME organizations that face major data loss & don't have disaster recovery close down within one year of operation.
- The year 2022 saw the highest number of Ransomware attacks in India.
- There is a 20% increase in Cyber Attacks YoY
- 40% of organizations have some kind of hybrid working environment, which means their data is more at risk.
- Common causes of data loss are hardware/system failure (31%), human error (29%) and viruses, and malware or Ransomware (29%).

These facts must have made it clear to you that no matter how safe you think you are, you are always at risk of a data loss disaster unless you have a Backup plan & system in place.

2

The 9 Transformational Habits

Habit #1

Consistently Question Your Mindset

At the Office: About Data Criticality & Backup/Restore.

At Home: About Family, being "taken for Granted", and support for getting Back up.

Here are some guideline questions to begin with when questioning your Mindset:

Does it occur to you that Data is the New OIL?

Also, begin by answering the "Why" of Data Management/ Backup in the 1st place (1st point of Mindset), similar to asking the Why of Everything that you and I all do before we can actually commit to it.

Answering the Why is the Question that brings "Focus and Results".

Ashutosh asked his CEO Mr. Ramakant Desai, "What were the different heads under which he could get the IT budget allocated for next year." Mr. Desai said, "It is your prerogative, IT comes under you, interact with finance, but one aspect is clear day-to-day Operations, Security, and Cloud should get priority."

Ashutosh replied, "Whatever best precautions and systems we take, employee/external man-made or natural disasters are bound to happen at some stage. The only aspect that can keep our data available under all circumstances for our critical operations is Backup".

CEO "That is a new mindset, we all have faced some personal disaster, and we take Backup plans like insurance to be prepared for it. I agree with your views; having a similar Backup plan would make sure that the organization is up and running in minimal time after any inevitable disaster."

Ashutosh," Business Continuity Plan from a Backup perspective is critical and one of the top 3 at any given time; I am delighted you approve of it. Let us create a workshop for key stakeholders. Who do you want to be part of it?".

A mindset starting with the self for data Criticality & Backup/restoration is the starting point and needs to be looked at daily. We live in quite a dynamic world where realities are consistently changing, so being alert and consistent is essential.

Ashutosh's infra Head Mrs. Sunita Reddy tells him, **"Boss, you are right about Mindset. I recall a news item, a lady lifting the side of a car much beyond her physical capacity, as her Mindset was to save her child at risk underneath the car. Whatever it takes, we want to have that kind of mindset".**

Ashutosh and the team also saw the "WHY" of data Backup. They understood the criticality of the Organizational Backup to keep it up and running at full capacity, even after any kind of data disaster.

The Family Scenario

Let's take a peek at Ashutosh talking with his personal life boss, his wife Sadhavi, about the car incident and Mindset. They both agreed that despite both being busy, they are both working for Families and would want their growing teenage children to develop the Mindset that Family comes first and is one of the top 2 priorities, even in the toughest scenario.

His better half added, "And the Why of Family is so clear, who would not want the people who love and support them and whom they love and support unconditionally in every phase of their life? These are the people who will be your Backup under every circumstance."

His Mom sitting beside them, added, "How about having a Backup Mindset for every aspect of life, whether it is work or Family? After all, nothing in life is ever certain. We really can't take Plan A for granted. Disaster can strike anytime, and we can be taken by surprise."

"Having a Backup Mindset would mean that we have Plan B/Plan C to fall back on. In fact, in the older days, when medical facilities in villages were not so good and mortality rates were high, people used to have multiple children as a Backup Plan because they knew that only a few of them would survive. And in those days, people were dependent on children in their old age completely, so having adult children was a must."

Ashutosh and his wife laughed heartily, amused at Mother's interesting analogy that emphasized the importance and criticality of Backup!

Habit #2

Identify and Involve Those Who Matter

At the Office: Involve those who bring in Money, Business people

At Home: Involve those who bring in unconditional Love, Children & Elders

Ashutosh calls for a meeting with the Production head Surinder Jha, along with Backup Subject Matter Expert, P.Venkat. He then proceeds to ask Mr. Jha about the system running in case of Disaster for his Operational Technology.

Mr. Jha says, "I have not changed my machines for almost 20-25 years, the OS are old, and you are not able to get us support for these. When failure/disaster happens, which for us is almost day-to-day, it takes us a hell of a lot of time to get the machines up and running again.

Additionally, we are scared to integrate as this might mean more issues through intranet & internet, overall the systems view is largely manual or legacy."

The Subject Matter Expert says, "Jha sir, 1st of all, let us understand your Operation Technology systems and what you wish to Backup based on your business requirements (OS, configuration, files, output thrown, performance) and the machines you have, I recall you already have some redundancies for OT.

Which ones are connected, partially connected or disconnected from each other when the Backup is required?

What RPO/RTO based on multiple parameters like minimal or frequent changes in the set of protocols."

"Actually, in a way, older systems in some cases have fewer chances of attacks as there are very few systems that Ransomware would want to attack, new kids on the block who mastermind these attacks don't know much about legacy systems."

"Then, of course, there are Backup technology partners who can:

- Support older OSs
- Work even on a stand-alone basis
- Throw centralized data even for unconnected machines

We could get your OT systems audited by experienced Backup focused partners; please give us your time options."

Next in line to meet up with is the Sales Head Mr. Chakraborti. Ashutosh, the Infra Head, Mrs. Sunita Reddy & the Backup Subject Matter Expert, P. Venkat are all sitting together and asking the Sales Head for his opinion and analysis. He says, "I cannot afford to lose even a single data point, and you said the cost for making sure we don't lose anything is way too high".

The Infra Head, Mrs. Sunita Reddy, reminds him, "Chakrabortijee, I recall during your QBR, your team lead said that for 40% of the product ranges, 10-20% of information missing out does not make a difference, let us analyze and look at where you need, what kind of system and when it comes to IT applications for dispatch & billing, we could give immediate availability of data, but that is not required for every piece of data point, correct?" "Let us look at what the system needs:

1. High Availability
2. 30 mins to 5 hours RTO
3. 6 hours to a few days RTO
4. A few mins to 1 day RPO"

Ashutosh continued his meetings with all departments, and all these Interactions with the different business groups led to a mutually agreeable, suitably budgeted Backup plan.

Remember that an optimized functional middle ground has to be found; the idealistic, most exhaustive Backup that everyone wants never ever materializes.

The required functional end result is what an organization and its business people demand at an optimal level.

Ashutosh said, "Since the beginning of setting up Data centers and Backup a best practice document was created to set priorities for each application in the environment. However, now we need to define them possibly in 3 categories from the business and hence, the Backup point of view. These categories would be **Critical, Important and Regular applications.**

Here is the definition of RPO/RTO for your ready reference.

- **The RPO (recovery point objective).** This term refers to the maximum allowable data loss rate. It is measured over a period of time and is generally staggered as follows: no data loss, 1, 4 or 24 hours of data.
- **The RTO (recovery time objective).** This refers to the maximum time that an application can remain down before it is restarted. The RTO is staggered in a manner similar to RPO: no delay, 1, 4 or 24 hours.

The Family Scenario

In the evening, when Ashutosh was talking with his young children & parents about what actions and behavior from him would make them happy. This is what they said,

Mother "*Beta,* once a week, 30 minutes of undivided attention from you gives us the most satisfaction; we understand that you have many responsibilities and are pressed for time. We also know you are a wonderful human and doing well. God Bless you".

Father "*Arre yaar, tu to bas yeh bata mujhe,* consistently *apni* health *ka Dyaan kaise rakhega, yeh pure din tera Bluetooth Ear me laga rehta hai,* wired one *he laga le, meri kuch baate toh maan liya kar, humara* to survival struggle *tha, tum kyo itna kaam karte ho.*"

{Broadly translated, it means: You tell me, son, how are you going to take care of your health consistently? You have your Bluetooth plugged into your ear the whole day. The least you could do is wear a wired one. Listen to me sometimes, at least. We struggled to survive, but you have everything; why do you work such long hours?}

Teenage Son "*Papa, aap to bus meri* life planning *sun liya karo*, and let us plan to see the cricket match happening in 2 months' time live together at the stadium."

{Papa, all I want is to share my life plan with you and also let's plan to see that cricket match happening in 2 months' time live together at the stadium.}

Daughter "Popsi, let us dance together to my favorite English Song. I'll make a video and tease my Bestie. You are my hero."

Ashutosh was so touched by all this. All these people showering such unconditional love on him, worrying about his health, wanting to include him in all aspects of their lives and having fun. All they asked for was his time and attention.

Habit #3

The Golden Rule

At the Office: Grand old 3-2-1 is now brand New 3-2-1-1-0.

At Home: 3 generations, 2 Gender balance, Husband – Wife, Zero Love lost.

It's a regular office day at work. The Finance Department head Manoj Chavan is a little upset with Ashutosh, "Same data, multiple copies, multiple locations, why so much of wastage Ashutosh jee, and you keep asking for more and more funds."

Ashutosh explained the criticality to him, "Manoj Jee, 3-2-1-1-0 is an industry-proven golden rule. We cannot afford to risk data under any circumstances. Can we take guarantee of no fire, natural disaster or hardware, man-made cyber security or internal threat despite all the precautions? Even the best of global security has been breached. 3-2-1-1-0 would make sure we have data available under all circumstances.

Here is the White Paper that our Backup Subject Matter Expert. Mr. P. Venkat has made.

3-2-1 has existed since the start of the early 2000s when given by US photographer Peter Krogh and is still the gold standard though it has been much refined now."

White Paper on 3-2-1-1-0

As per the latest best practice, the optimal Backup strategy is the "3-2-1-1-0" principle. This means:

- Having 3 copies of your data
- These copies should be stored on 2 different media to avoid loss, corruption, or hacking (ransomware attack).
- 1 copy should be stored offsite and one offline or cloud, both immutable (**immutability means that this copy cannot be modified in any way, under any circumstances**).
- Zero Errors on Backup

With this strategy, you can protect yourself against almost all kinds of data loss risks – which can occur in any scenario.

Though data centers exist even under the ocean and a data permanence kind of scenario appears possible for future generations in case of real extreme scenarios, that, for now, is beyond the scope of this book.

To give you a better idea of this Backup strategy, let me take company X as an example.

- Company X is an SME running an online store where customers order kits to create their own coffee capsules.

- It, therefore, produces critical information that it must protect, such as its customers' personal data. To do this, it has chosen to create:
  - ❖ A Backup of its data exists in Delhi on a server.
  - ❖ And an external one-on-prem storage/Cloud storage. Both immutable.
  - ❖ Another Backup exists on a remote server located in Kolkata.

Hence 3 copies, 2 media, 1 off-site, 1 offline or cloud & zero errors on Backup every single time– to be followed totally.

In the event of an incident on the Delhi site, the data can be found on the server in Kolkata.

Although the chances of such an incident occurring are minimal, if both servers are destroyed, the external on-prem storage or cloud storage will restore the data on a new server.

This minimizes the risk of data being lost centrally on the same site and media.

It is recommended to use cloud Backup with intelligence & based on need analysis, though now almost all kinds of organizations (even Government, Pharma, Insurance, Fintech, FMCG, Retail, Manufacturing, etc.) are trusting cloud for some kind of data, if not all.

IT professionals should continue to demonstrate caution with what to move when moving data to cloud. The need for caution is especially true in the case of Backup data, as the organization is essentially renting idle storage.

Although cloud Backup provides an attractive upfront price point, long-term cloud costs can add up. **Repeatedly paying for the same 100 TBs of data eventually becomes more expensive than owning 100 TB of storage.**

It was found in the latest survey that 94% of Ransomware attacks targeted Backup repositories, with 68% of those being successful. Hence one offline Backup and one on cloud seems to be a good choice.

The Family Scenario

That day, after explaining the importance of the 3-2-1-1-0 to the finance head when Ashutosh went home, he carried the thought with him and decided to use it constructively to build his wife side family relationships stronger.

While sitting with his wife over a cup of coffee, he said to her, "We typically have affection with one generation up and one generation down, and as husband and wife, we have gender balance in terms of Male/Female, and this is great for the growth of our emotional quotient.

And at any stage, if there is Zero love with anybody, we should make all effort for it to be re-established without any delay for natural relationship maintenance. This includes your and my parents and siblings; let us have a family get-together of both sets of parents, siblings and children in the next 30 days. This Is our Family, and we need to nurture it."

While having loads of fun at the get-together, they created a new paradigm for the Family Tree:

The Earlier Family Paradigm

Family 3-2-1 Earlier: (3) generations - Grandparents, parents and children, (2) Husband & Wife. (1) Family, only with Girls trained that after marriage, their parental Home and Family are no longer a priority; they are taught to consider only the marital Home and in-laws as their priority largely. While the boy never really considered his in-laws as part f his family.

The New Family 2.0 Paradigm

Family 3-2-1-1-0 now: (3) Generations [Parents, Husband & Wife & Children], (2) Husband -Wife- (1-1) Equality, both wife/husband side of the Family being considered as own, (0) and **if loss of love in any part, it should be restored in no time.**

This was the way it was in our ancient Indian culture also, later, it degenerated with other influences.

While cleaning up after the wonderful get-together, they were tired but happy, and his wife said to him playfully, "*Kya baat hai*, tum to *bilkul* transform *ho rahe ho*" [This is great, you are getting totally transformed]. "I never imagined this could happen to my husband after 17 years of marriage. We are all delighted with this new you."

Habit #4

Always Question The Relevance

At the Office: Use Backup for Backup only

At Home: Relevance of Old Habits/Customs/Assets/Plan

Question the Relevance of data backed up,

Backup Vs Archival

Don't use Backup for data retention.

Let's get into a conversation where Ashutosh says to Finance Head Manoj Jee, "I recall you mentioning about minimizing Backup data; we re-looked and found that **most organizations retain data within their Backups for far too long.**

Legally we don't need much, and whatever is required could be done through Archival".

Manoj then asks him the difference between Backup and Archival. Ashutosh goes on to explain.

"**Backup:** Data which is in primary storage and a copy overall or de-duplicated is available in Backup."

"**Archival:** Data which is moved to Secondary storage is removed from Primary storage, and the overall infra required to manage storage also comes down".

Manoj Chavan is impressed, "Wow, How much we would be able to save."

Ashutosh answers him, "Possibly 20-35% reduction to begin with and the more data contained within the Backup infrastructure, the more difficult it is to manage and analyze and the more expensive it becomes. That would also bring some savings possibly, but I would like to put the initial figure to be around 20% in overall storage and related infra. Long-term retention beyond 5 years is required for the board, and MCA for Accounts books would be kept in low-cost LTO at 2 locations. This would also mean we could get them whenever we want".

The Family Scenario

Relevance of Old Habits/Customs/Assets/Plan

That very evening, while they were watching a documentary together, 16-year-old Samarth asked his Papa, "Why do you still not let us cut our nails in the evening and also, why don't men cook in the Home? It would be lovely to have food cooked by you as well. Let's both do it together; it would be good fun". We should even make it a regular practice to contribute to housework.

Ashutosh was impressed, and he saw it as the perfect time and avenue for changing old paradigms that were no longer valid; He said, "Why not? Let us re-look at old customs, habits and even old material lying in our Home for consistently causing workability; this Sunday breakfast I am cooking, and you can cut nails whenever you want; we have enough lights even at night at home Also, let's make a roster for chipping in with household chores equally as Shambavi also works full time."

Habit #5

Protect & Safeguard Your Extensions

At the Office: Why is some infra orphaned/not backed up?

At Home: Why Extended Family & Close Friends are not given enough importance?

The Backup Subject Matter Expert, P. Venkatesh questions Ashutosh, "Endpoints and cloud SaaS applications are not backed up, 3 critical persons left the organization in the last 1 month and deleted their data from the common file server as well. We need to address this."

"Check their Laptops; we should be able to get even deleted data restored from their HDD."

This worked, but Ashutosh knew that backing up Critical Endpoints and Cloud SaaS applications, including O365, sales force, and other applications hosted on cloud was definitely required.

Endpoints

Laptops, desktops, tablets and smartphones – all contain valuable data that might be uniquely stored on them. It is reasonable to assume that data created on these devices might never be stored in a data center storage device unless they are specifically backed up and that data will be lost if the endpoint fails, is lost or is stolen. The good news is that endpoint protection **is more practical than ever, thanks to the multiple cloud & on-prem solutions.**

Backup, in any case, is required and needs to be evaluated.

For endpoints, Laptop/Desktop Backup is required because of the following:

- They contain the most recently worked on data for the organization.
- These systems, since they go out of office, are most at risk, as per almost all relevant studies.
- Some kind of hybrid working means that data in work-from-home or remote locations are much more at risk.
- Business/compliance requirements might suffer if the data were to be lost.
- Senior most persons are more mobile and have more valuable organizational data.

Ashutosh called a meeting with the Infra Head, Mrs. Sumita Reddy & Backup Subject Matter Expert, Mr. P. Venkat, "I need both of you to prepare a detailed report on Infra not being Backed Up and specific reasons why they are not required to be Backed Up."

Here's the Report prepared by the Internal Team along with the Cloud Service Provider:

The majority of Cloud application providers are clear (though some don't say it clearly for their own reasons) that 3rd party backup solutions are critically required for their applications.

For example, One of the world's largest cloud application providers, "Salesforce" (CRM market leader) themselves, says.

1. "There are a number of data Backup solutions offered by our partners on our AppExchange. Some of these are more comprehensive in that they allow you to automate backups of both your data AND your metadata and provide a mechanism by which to restore that data easily. **You can search for these by visiting AppExchange directly and searching for keyword backup.** We recommend that customers vet multiple offerings and audit the reviews provided by other customers before selecting one of these offerings."
2. "Even with the best of intentions, users and administrators have been in situations where they have either deleted large amounts of data or have modified records, only to later realize that a mistake was made. With tools like the Data Loader, it is very easy to mass delete or update records. And a simple mistake in your source file or field mapping could spell Disaster for your data. It is recommended that you keep a regular backup of your data and do a manual point-in-time backup before you proceed with any major data project within your organization."

   Accidental deletion remains the top cause of Salesforce data loss, **leading to nearly 70% of data loss incidents.**

Even otherwise, SaaS application experts say that.

1. Look at the RTO objective

2. The cost involved in recovery
3. Days after which deleted data is permanently gone(if it remains available after deletion)

Apart from the above points, Google Drive/One Drive/ iCloud Drive are shared storage and, at best, part of the Backup strategy and not the primary Backup tool even for Endpoints (forget about server & large storage backup) because.

1. It has only one copy of data at the central location, with source intentional or accidental deletion target is bound to go away at max after few days; who is monitoring this?
2. What about users who leave the organization?
3. Cyberattacks
4. No organization control largely for this individual-controlled data
5. Drills for audit and restoration are not very practical
6. Regulatory requirements of data available for lots of Industries, BFSI, and Health, to name a few
7. No snapshots or data across your machine based on the selection
8. eDiscovery is not possible for business differentiators and compliance with standards like GDPR.
9. Organizations themselves are responsible for data and security, not Google/MS/Apple

There are all kinds of solutions suiting multiple requirements of Endpoints and SaaS-based solutions, including individual data privacy, even from the IT admin team with continuous data protection instead of scheduled data protection.

These are capable of anywhere web restore and live PST backup using One Drive/Google Drive for Backup, meaning there is no need to use BW to move data/central IT team control.

The humungous data erosion & acceptability of cloud by a majority of organizations in the last decade, more so in the last 5 years, has created multiple challenges, including data security, manageability, storage scaling etc., for organizations, and made companies shift to cloud with SaaS solutions like O365, Salesforce, Tally on cloud etc.

The majority of these organizations think that these SaaS providers, especially from big MNCs, already have high availability, and there is no need for us to Back up. **Though most of these cloud SaaS solutions have clearly mentioned in fine print that Backup** is the responsibility **of the client,** yet the client expects the data from cloud-based SaaS providers.

As per the ESG Report in 2021,

https://www.esg-global.com/hubfs/ESG-Infographic-DP-for-SaaS.pdf

- 33% of organizations solely rely on SaaS vendors to protect their SaaS-resident data.
- 55% of organizations have lost SaaS-resident data in the past 12 months.

This data is critical from the business, legal as well as compliance point of view.

And SaaS storages are not centrally managed and are controlled by individuals largely.

There are solutions that use these SaaS storages and yet provide control to the central IT team.

A number of generic users, such as desktops/laptops, could be Backed up using One Drive/Google Drive as data is not too critical for the organization.

Also, some cloud applications which guarantee data availability need not be Backed up.

However, all servers to be Backed up in some way for sure.

IN THE NEXT MEETING: The team requests Ashutosh, "Let us look at critical Laptop/Desktop & O365 Backup, as well as Salesforce Backup."

The Family Scenario

Why are extended Family & close friends not given enough importance?

This entire episode of some critical data being left orphaned without Backup made Ashutosh think about reviewing where he was doing the same in his personal life.

Thinking on this deeply made him realize that while he had taken steps to ensure that he did not neglect his immediate Family, he was still not giving enough time and importance to his extended Family and friends. And how they had always been a great support system to him.

That same evening he called Atul, his maternal cousin whom he related to as his real brother since childhood and said, "Bhai, we have not talked for ages. My apologies, let us catch up for coffee, next Wednesday I will be close to your office, let us meet at 6.30 PM".

After the phone call, Ashutosh immediately put on his to-do list a catch-up meeting with one extended family member or close friend every week. He decided life is too short not to meet up with those who Back you up unconditionally.

Habit #6

It's All About The Money!

At the Office: Think about the Business Value (Monetization) of your Data & IT.

At Home: Address Financial Aspects as well.

CEO to Ashutosh "Though I like you a lot, I have a complaint to make." Ashutosh was taken aback, "*Aab maine kya kar diya*"? [What have I done now?]

CEO- "I want you to think why organizations exist; I am sure you know they exist for profit through touching people's life positively. If you don't contribute in that you cannot grow beyond a point, IT is no longer a support, but it is a differentiating function for organizational transformation, so even you need to think business."

Ashutosh was inspired by this, and he said, "That is great, now onwards, I will come up with different ideas about how IT can use data to make more profits."

He took it forward and told his team, "Let us start looking at the business side of IT and data which the majority of IT persons don't have the time and vision to look at. This will get us all growth and attention within the organization, and wherever else we go."

"We should brainstorm on what our organization could do with data to accomplish what it is up to and then expand on that further for ideas in profitable and viable new directions."

"We would also look at what each one of our organization department (Marketing, Sales, Finance, Production, After sales support, Customer Happiness,....) could do with data".

"Competition Analysis".

"This will bring our creative side out."

The Family Scenario

Address Financial Aspects as well

The next morning at the office, the SME expert asked Ashutosh, "Boss, yesterday we talked about the financial aspect of IT & data, and it was an eye opener. Now I feel motivated to look at the financial side of my personal life as well."

Ashutosh laughed and jokingly asked, "Are you asking for a raise in the midst of the year?"

The Backup Subject Matter Expert, Mr. P. Venkat replied, "Is that the only way to increase earnings? You seem to have managed your money well right from the beginning. Could you support the team in learning to manage their money well by investing in avenues of their choice? You could train them informally."

Ashutosh enthusiastically said, "Why not, for sure."

Inspired by this and in order to guide his team well on managing and growing their money wisely, began reviewing his own financial resources, needs and decisions.

He reviewed things like

Family needs for children's studies, their old age money needs, passive income, the money required for health, vacations, and financial goals by which he would not need to work for money any longer than the next 5 years.

He would have financially abundance for the life-long requirements of his family within the next 5 years. He would no longer need to work for money any longer; he would be working purely for the passion of working to create an impact.

Then he began teaching his staff, wife, and children about financial planning and management, making them responsible for their own life rather than dependent on anybody, not even him. That way, they would blossom at work when they have financial freedom.

Habit #7

Structure & Measurability

At the Office: Bring Structure to your Unstructured data- Unstructured Data Planning, IOT, CCTV, Research, Scan docs, Audio, Video Data.

At Home: Love and Care- Devise ways to bring measurability to this unmeasurable parameter

Another day in Ashutosh's life, Ashutosh to IT Infra Head:

"Unstructured data is going into multiple PBs and exploding at a 30% compounded rate, we have tonnes of storage, multiple file systems, and then there is our critical research, CCTV & IoT data. Lots of money is being poured into all this. All this could prove to be major data for the organization, and it could be monetized or analyzed for the organization's benefit, but it appears very difficult to manage."

The IT infra head replied calmly, "I know a few specialized organizations that are considered to be experts in this field. Even large Global System Integrators, M&E Organizations, Research Labs, Spiritual Organizations, and Educational Organizations use them across the globe; they seem to know all the ways to":

1. Archive/Backup/Migrate/Sync between multiple diverse storages going up to low-cost LTO & even cloud.

2. No loss of compatibility and ACLs (right management).
3. Data integrity assurance.
4. Integrated workflow with our IT systems through API/ XML/web services.
5. Multiple file system support.
6. Metatags (Manual & Automatic) & low-res previews for Movie/Audio files.
7. Unlimited scalability up to 100s of PBs.
8. Possibility of extensive reporting on the top.
9. Integration with multiple business applications.
10. Creation of business applications like Media Asset Management or Social Media Application Management, which multiple business people could think of.

Ashutosh was excited, amazed and relieved all at once, "Wow, let us call them. It seems that this impression that unstructured data is not manageable by mid-size organizations is a myth, of-course regular OEMs managing Backup do seem not to have the technology to manage it."

The Family Scenario

That evening, Ashutosh was really excited and told his father, "Papa, although we are interacting and bonding more and more as a family, still, some days, our love and care scorecard is low. Let us work to see how we can improve upon this; maybe we can build a system or set guidelines and activities for this."

In response to his suggestion, Papa & his wife created some practices for encouraging and measuring love & care like

1. A Quarterly family picnic.
2. A Weekly creative fun time.
3. Breakfast together to the extent possible by everybody.
4. All who are available at Home to have meals together.
5. How many times every one is to laugh minimum in a day.

Habit #8

Play By The Rules

At the Office: Plan, Execute & Analyze Business Continuity Plan/DR runbooks from a Backup Point of View.

Criticality of it when Disaster strikes or even day to day

At Home: Rule Book for running family smoothly

Board Member to Ashutosh:

"We have got this Business Continuity Plan from an IT perspective rule book report made by consultant Daman Dev Sood; please get this implemented if there are gaps in the way we are doing it."

Ashutosh "Wow, I am delighted. This will make things simpler for Venkat and his team."

Report: Business Continuity Plan from a Backup Point of View.

An organization is an independent entity, by its very name, designed to run forever, irrespective of individuals and circumstances.

Business continuity means that the business continues under all circumstances, i.e., natural and man-made disasters, right from personnel and assets (including but not limited to Data). Having a Succession Plan for management & key persons is essential for the smooth continuance of the business.

Also, as earthquakes, tsunamis and the coronavirus have shown us, Natural Disaster Management and Pandemic Management have become a critical part of the business mix.

Additionally, Cashflow Management, HR Management for key people and Entire Infrastructure Management (including Plant and Machinery) are much needed too.

Business Continuity Plan from the IT side includes all the IT Applications/Infrastructure/Responsibilities (Manpower) working to deliver the desired outcome under all circumstances—no single point of failure from hardware Infra, Cloud, Security, Power, and Applications availability.

Business Continuity Plan, from the Backup point of view, would be focused on the detailed "**Why**" of Backup, resulting in "**What**" to accomplish from Backup, giving an output of Backup infra & manpower. It would mean having clear and detailed Policies, Guidelines and End to End Rule Book for what aspects and steps to cover for a Business Continuity Plan.

This means increase in Backup frequency **needs** to be discussed and planned. Because of Ransomware, data centers must increase the frequency of Backups — once a night is no longer enough. **All data sets should be protected multiple times per day.**

The most common recoveries are not disaster recoveries; they are recoveries of a single file or single application.

Occasionally IT needs to recover from a failed storage system, but it is extremely rare that IT needs to recover from a full disaster where the entire data center is lost.

Organizations, of course, still must plan for the possibility of this type of recovery.

How to adapt your disaster recovery plan

Critical Application: RPO & RTO=0

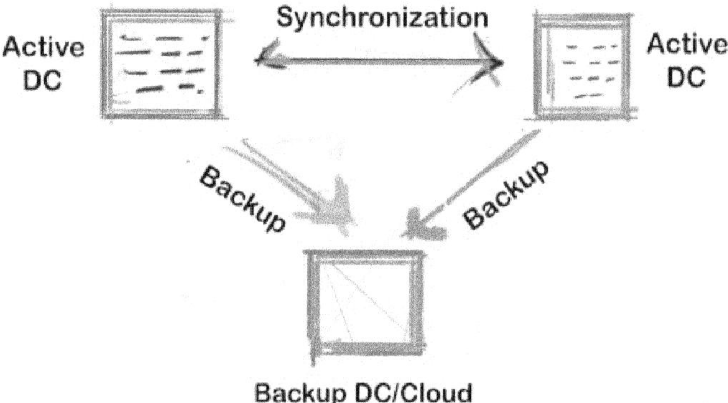

The company cannot function without these applications. It runs its application:

- In 2 data centers.
- With spaces of several kilometers (+100km apart).
- Data is synced between the two locations.
- Backups are placed in a third data center/Cloud.

Essential Applications: RPO>1 hour & RRO>4 hours

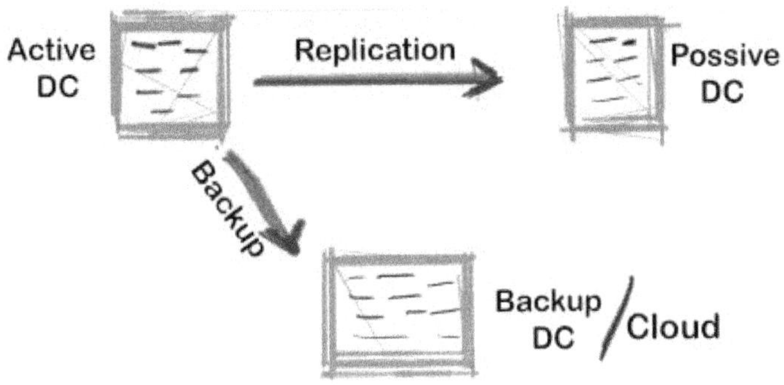

The company can function without these applications, but not for more than an hour. It runs its application:

- In a primary data center.
- The data is replicated in a second location, several kilometers apart (+100km).
- Backups are located in a third data center/Cloud.

Non-critical application: RPO>24 hours & RTO> 24 hours

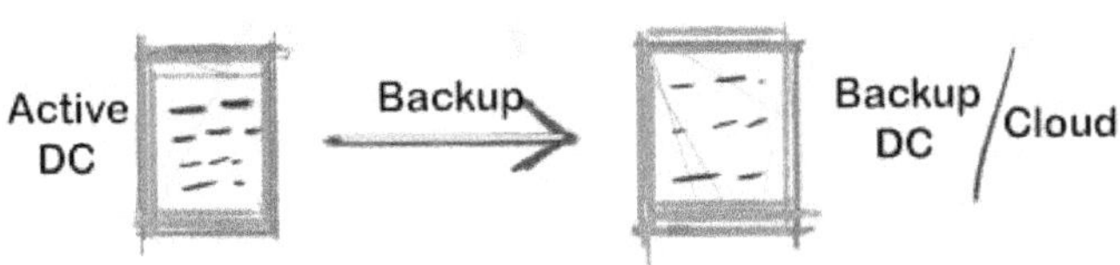

The company can function without this application for more than a day. It runs its application:

- In a data center.

- Data backups are located in a second data center or cloud.

It will use the Backups to restore the application to the second data center if the first is down.

Detailed Business Continuity Plan document from Backup perspective is made based on:

- Business requirement for appropriate RPO/RTO after detailed analysis
- 3-2-1-1-0 approach to create Backup required, details about how this is being implemented.
- Roles and responsibility matrix for the Backup team with Backup even among them.
- Specification making, options analyzed & finalization of requisite automation tools for Backup and recovery and implementation.
- Consistent partial restoration drills for requisite RPO/ RTO and frequency of this based on application criticality and transition.
- Monitoring of all these processes being fully followed.
- Consistent review of all the above for any changes so required.

Few specialized organizations, as a result of their experience of decades, have created assessments and documentation in detail to support where they stand in terms of Business Continuity Plan runbooks from a Backup perspective, current business requirements study for Backup, RPO/RTO current and required, what are the gaps and the way to fill those, revised Business Continuity Plan Runbooks from Backup perspective recommendations and even implementation of these gaps.

To help customers set up their Business Continuity Plan from a Backup perspective, we offer iBART (itSimple Backup Archival Restoration Testing) service providing consulting and an engineered approach.

iBART does a deep-dive assessment of your Business Continuity Plan from Backup perspective strategies and Backup practices, which helps you create a Backup Mindset & drastically minimize the impact of incidents on your business and possibly prevent data loss resulting from any kind of data interruptions.

The Family Scenario

That day, when Ashutosh reached home, he eagerly told his wife, "We have created a detailed rule book for Backup in the organization for data. It will help us function smoothly, and everyone will know what to do by following the practices listed."

His wife said, "Why not create a similar one for the Family as well? You end up eating much more sugar than you should and sleeping less than required. Our Daughter's timeline of sleep is erratic; I end up not spending time at my own office as I get busy with other aspects."

Ashutosh enthusiastically agreed, "Let us all sit together and make it happen next month during vacation time. How wonderful it will be to have a Rule Book of our Family, each and every aspect, made democratically with a dash of authority from parents in a few critical areas, and agreed upon and followed by all".

Habit #9

Think Future

At the Office: Think Future for Data Backup

At Home: Think Future for Family

CEO to Ashutosh: "You would be glad to know about the new initiative; we have hired the Best IT consultants (they are working with our global competitors for the future direction, and IT is a critical part of that). To my surprise, they included your current favourite Backup as well."

Ashutosh: "Wow, you made my day. It will make it easier for me to create a roadmap for years ahead, and as you mentioned Backup, let me tell you, despite the fact that Backup seems to be quite an old technology, which appears to have stabilized with hardly any new development but the truth is that even in this area there is expected to be lots of changes like in every IT field which is quite dynamic."

"Traditionally data Backup and recovery used to be a very simple process. But today, data is generated and distributed across highly complex ecosystems, e.g. customization of cloud applications, Multi-cloud, GDPR, global privacy laws, big data, containerized /Dockers workloads, edge, IoT in distributed locations with minimal local infra, Hybrid working, making data Backup and recovery more difficult to achieve and requires the adoption of Backup strategy differently."

Following are a few of the Backup and recovery trends:

1. **Multi-cloud data Backup & recovery:** Multi-cloud data Backup and recovery solutions can Backup data across cloud services from different providers. Often, these solutions take Backups from one service and store those Backups on another for disaster recovery purposes. Ideally, these solutions should also enable recovery for different providers.
2. **Hybrid Cloud Backups:** Like multi-cloud deployments, hybrid clouds can grant greater flexibility and control to organizations and are growing in popularity. Hybrid cloud Backup solutions are an option that you can use to either create a hybrid cloud or to support a hybrid cloud that is already in place.
3. **Cloud-Native Backup & disaster recovery:** As more organizations adopt cloud-only environments, cloud-native Backup and recovery methods are increasingly necessary. These solutions are built into cloud services and are typically offered directly by providers. Cloud-native solutions can enable you to easily automate Backups, manage Backups at scale, and recover workloads and data globally with ease. These solutions are particularly important for cloud-native applications.
4. **Continuous Backup:** To ensure granularity without impacting production performance, the future of Backup is moving from periodic Backup to continuous Backup. Combining always-on replication and granular recovery enables continuous data protection that allows you to move away from the periodic point-in-time copies used in traditional Backup technology. If an

outage occurs at 17:26, Continuous Data Protection can restore data from 17:25 rather than from a Backup that is probably at least 4 hours old—with all the data written since the 12:30 snapshot permanently lost.

5. **Unstructured data PB to EB at distributed places having lots of business value to be derived dominated by big players.** M&E, Medical, CCTV footage, Social media, IoT. The Backup, migration, Archival and Synch of this would become more and more typical as growth is highest here. One of the critical aspects being what to keep and what not to keep and adding on business applications for integration, workflow and business analysis.

In today's times, you also need to account for Data Privacy Laws & how to take Backup differently, keeping in mind aspects like the Right to be forgotten; these laws are there in 71% of countries, 14% in the process of being drafted including in India, this would be a big Game Changer. It requires you to know:

- Which PII (Personal Identifiable Information) is lying in which system?
- How is sensitive information being taken care of, and are they appropriately masked?
- Is the eDiscovery of PII required?
- What can be done to take care of the Right to be Forgotten?
- Understanding the localization of PII storage.

The Family Scenario

Ashutosh talked with his children too on the same lines that day, "We have a decent amount of data at home as well, which is scattered around; this includes photos, passwords, assets, stock market/mutual fund & other investments, partially made will or No will. It is essential to take care of it, and we should also plan for the Family's long-term future for profession, health, finances etc."

His son replied: "We all are here for each other for the long term, and some of it is well managed on cloud drives, and why to bother about the long term? It will sort itself out and be taken care of; why bother about money, we are quite well off."

Ashutosh counselled his son, giving him an example, "My grandpa was filthy rich in Pakistan, but he died early, the family had to migrate during partition, leaving all the assets back there and with no long-term planning & insurances, my grandma who was largely uneducated had a difficult time managing, and the family went through a serious financial mess. Your saying we are quite well off makes me really concerned, as each generation needs to be capable, plan, earn, and consistently excel independently too, no matter how well supported they may be financially, otherwise any problem or crisis could throw them in the deep seas of trouble."

Daughter & Son together chimed in, "Oops, we never knew this!"

Learning from this, the Family decided to create a long-term plan, including:

A. Each member of the family visioning what future they foresee for themselves & the family in 20 years, 10 years, 5 years and 1 year down the line in alignment with each other.

B. What is required in terms of skills, funds and people?

C. Arrangements for education/training, life & health insurance to cover all kinds of eventualities.

D. Financial planning, including making each other aware of all individual & joint investments etc.

E. Making the wills of all the adult family members accessible to a few chosen family members and one trustworthy chosen person outside the family.

F. Managing data in a manner to facilitate availability at all times, including documents, finances, memories and heirlooms.

G. A periodic review of skills, investments made and those required.

3

How Come One Habit is Enough?

CEO to Ashutosh: "These Backup habits have become the Tail of Hanuman [too long]. There is no end, one after another. It seems to be taking up all your time. What is happening with your new responsibility around strategic planning that you were handle along with the CFO, KPMG and our most competent independent board member Mr. Dhiren Desai?"

Ashutosh: "Boss, we have talked about this with all stakeholders of strategic planning, and we all agree that we wish to create a Backup mindset in all our strategic planning and a Backup mindset/culture of Org."

CEO: "WHAT??? Are you kidding? This IT backup in the serious business of strategic planning, Culture and Mindset is just too much. I am having second thoughts about your role beyond IT."

Ashutosh: "Boss, relax. Trust me; all this came from Mr. Desai only 4 days back after my brief interactions with them about what we are doing in IT Backup; what he said is that all of us in the organization should have an open Mindset about ways to cause workability in every accountability that we have."

"It is foolish to expect different/more productive output with the same Mindset inputs; if we were to have Backup Mindset, we would be 100% focused on Plan A but open to other plans B/Plan C if Plan A does not work out."

"Even shifting people from one accountability to another based on what they show their inclination or suitability toward. Multiple strategies would be given by the vision that we have defined rather than what we have been doing so far."

"We see our 3-year plan profitability projection going up by 25% more than earlier with 2 more additions in the product line and becoming Number one in minimum 1 more niche category than we projected earlier."

CEO: "Are you sure?"

Ashutosh: "Yes, boss, here is Mr. Desai's detailed report."

CEO: "That's unbelievable. I was just kidding a while back; you are becoming a really amazing asset to the management. Well done, really amazing work."

Ashutosh: "To top it all, As per Mr. Desai, we should look at Mindset as a critical habit that is the root of all habits. If we are clear about creating something great and have a clear-cut mindset, then we go to whatever extent/options are required for that."

"A great analogy would be the way we Indians go to any extent to take care of our children's education, even much beyond our capacity. We do whatever options are required in terms of effort or money. It is not difficult because that is our default programming, our cultural mindset; it comes naturally to us."

"Similarly, it is not complex in the case of Backup; we can bring in a huge shift based on one HABIT OF BACKUP MINDSET in IT or beyond. And he advised us to create a poster with all 9 habits with comparisons about the same at home for easy reference and as reminders to implement these habits."

"These posters will be displayed throughout the organization if you approve the same. Even my MOM agrees with this."

CEO: "Hmm, a major topic for discussion in the next board meeting; let us prepare for this accomplishment to be shown to all. I am sure you agree that I gave you lots of input and groomed you beyond IT in the last few years; you have a bright future ahead of you."

Ashutosh: "It is all thanks to your support and blessings, Boss. I really appreciate DIL SE."

5 days ago at Home

Ashutosh, sitting at Home with his wife, sister Renu and Ma, "I am getting too confused about these habits and structuring; I think it is not going in the right direction. What do I do?"

Sadhavi to all "We are all making this too complicated, I was talking with Renu Didi and Ma, and we all think that not Doing & Actions but Mindset is one Critical Habit for any major Result that one wishes to cause beyond the ordinary.

Let us all focus on this one habit to cause the rest of them. Each day let us question ourselves: Is Family and our importance to each other one of the 1st two top priorities for each of us? This should drive us in the right direction and suitable actions.

In addition, having a pictorial representation of all the habits in each room at home will be a constant reminder to keep us on the right track."

Ashutosh: "My CEO calls you Mrs. Wise Lady & the 3 of you the critical pillars of my life for all the right reasons. He says that he is giving me all these extended roles thanks to you only. I am really blessed that I have the 3 of you in my life, along with all the other critical family members."

Summary of the 9 Critical Habits that Ashutosh Created with His Family & Office Colleagues

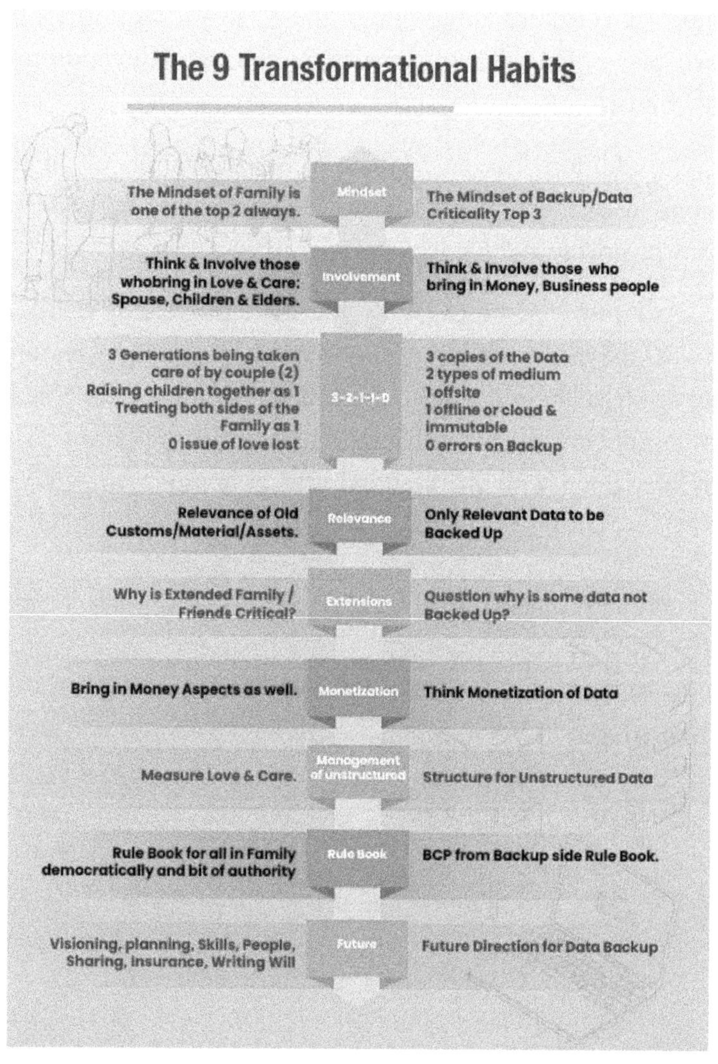

Download the latest Poster Link:
www.itsimple.in/MrBackup2

Family 2.0	Habit	Backup 2.0
1. The Mindset of Family is one of the top 2 always.	Mindset	The Mindset of Backup/Data Criticality Top 3
2. Think & Involve those who bring in Love & Care: Spouse, Children & Elders.	Involvement	Think & Involve those who bring in Money: Business people
3. (3) Generations being taken care of by couple (2) Raising children together as (1) Treating both sides of the Family as (1) (0) issues of love lost	3-2-1-1-0	3 copies of the Data 2 types of medium 1 offsite 1 offline or cloud & immutable 0 errors on Backup
4. Relevance of Old Customs/ Material/Assets.	Relevance	Only Relevant Data to be Backed Up
5. Why are Extended Family & Friends Critical?	Extensions	Question why is some data not Backed Up?
6. Bring in Money Aspects as well.	Monetization	Think Monetization of Data
7. Measure Love & Care	Management of unstructured	Structure for Unstructured Data
8. Rule Book for all in Family democratically with a dash of authority	Rule Book	Business Continuity Plan from Backup side Rule Book.
9. Future Plan including Visioning, Planning, Skilling, Safety net, Education, Insurance, Will Writing	Future	Future Direction for Data Backup

4

Going The Extra Mile: Sustainability/ ESG, Business Continuity Plan/ Resilience & Backup

Ashutosh to CEO: "I wish to take another responsibility. The other day you mentioned sustainability/ESG being key for the organization in front of investors. Kanwaljeeet Singh, DGM (IT), thinks that ESG, Business Continuity Plan/ Resilience & Backup could all be greatly co-related."

CEO: "I did not get this. Could you explain, is not your plate already quite full?"

Ashutosh: "We have our veteran expert Mr. Daman Dev Sood who has worked in Business Continuity Planning for us for years. Kanwaljeet & Daman Jee have discussed this at length, and Damanjee created a white paper. Let me show you that."

Ashutosh continues, "Looking at all the definitions & other aspects of white paper, The strong backup mindset in the organization, the Mindset trained to look at ways to cause workability under all circumstances in the short term as well as the long term could take care of Sustainability/ESG, Business

Continuity Plan/BCM as well as Backup. Though the main focus is long term".

CEO: "Are we not making it too simple? How would this critical aspect work out? This is becoming too serious from investors' point of view; it is a matter of the organization's future."

Ashutosh: "I understand it; Backup overall is a serious area, boss. The focus is on making organization in line with your favourite quote, "When the going gets tough, the tougher get going" The species like Dianasours, which could not adapt or train to get Back up in the face of disasters, became extinct. We need to support Mother Earth to have plans B & C for getting back in shape, which it has a natural capability for. Disasters/problems need to be anticipated and planned with multiple options and points of view. The sustainability of organizations and Earth have got to be perfectly in Sync." "With your approval, we will create a specialized team with.

- A couple of internal persons to be trained on ESG & Business Continuity Plan
- Rights to sit with the steering committee of almost all departments once a month minimum
- Possibly we would even hire one specialized person over a period of time

Damanjee has agreed to go the extra mile with us on this."

On the Family Front

That evening, Ashutosh was really excited, and his 16 y son Sambhav was in a mood to discuss, "Papa, how is your new backup mindset project going?"

Ashutosh: "We have included new futuristic Business Continuity Planning and Sustainability also in that, let us make family habits also in such a way that we remain a reputed family even in the generations to come,"

Sambhav: "Tell me more about this" After a bit of discussion, he got excited and told "Papa, how about we have a Sustainability/Business Continuity Plan talk in our neighbourhood, and we in the Family use resources at bare minimal levels on specific days, like no Screens days, switching off Lights/Fans, no Internet after 10 PM for all including you."

Ashutosh: "Excellent, Let us also talk about how short-term and long-term problems in the family could be anticipated and minimized. Let us create an emergency kit with essential supplies & cash and even do some unplanned drills."

Daman Dev Sood Report on Sustainability/ESG, Business Continuity Plan/BCM & BACKUP

https://www.damandevsood.com

Definitions

"The United Nations (UN) defines Sustainability as development that meets the needs of the present without compromising the ability of future generations to meet their own needs. Which could be a business continuity plan for earth, as the business of earth is sustaining lives on it."

ISO 22301 (the global standard for Business Continuity Management) defines Business Continuity Planning (Business Continuity Plan) as the "Capability of an organization to continue the delivery of products and services within acceptable time frames at predefined capacity during a disruption (ISO 22301: 2019)" Though it could include business continuity under all circumstances covering all critical aspects of the organization.

Disaster: as per Wikipedia, A disaster is a serious problem occurring over a short or long period of time that causes widespread human, material, an economic or environmental loss which exceeds the ability of the affected community or society to cope using its own resources. All the Disasters which come have one thing in common in the last 100 years or so. Their actual origin or magnitude, to a large extent is determined by the efforts of humans. Natural, Cyber, Economic, and Pandemic could be types of this.

Disasters that had a big impact on Sustainability & Business Continuity Plans where a Backup Mindset could have helped (reference www.researchgate.com):

1. Union Carbide's Bhopal plant disaster, where a methyl isocyanate gas leak resulted in over 15,000 deaths, is an example of a process design flaw.
2. 2010: British Petroleum oil rig, Deepwater Horizon, experienced a massive explosion; 11 workers died. Deepwater drilling on all oil rigs in the Gulf was

suspended, BP set up a compensation fund of $20 billion for reimbursement of losses, and early in the spill, the firm's stock had lost $88 billion in value, the failure of the blowout preventer, supposedly a control, enabled the resulting oil spill in the BP Deepwater.

3. 2005 Hurricane Katrina struck the Gulf Coast of the United States. In terms of physical damage, economic loss, and human impact, Hurricane Katrina was among the worst storms in US history. Category 3 was less severe in magnitude than many other hurricanes. Yet two contributing factors exacerbated its effects, both caused by human actions.

The concept of Sustainability recognizes that the world's resources are finite (there is only one Earth) and that human activities must be managed in a way that does not deplete them or damage the environment beyond repair. This requires a shift from short-term thinking and a focus on immediate profits towards a more holistic approach that considers the long-term implications of our actions.

The UN has identified 17 Sustainable Development Goals (SDGs) that provide a framework for global efforts to promote Sustainability.

These goals are interconnected and provide a roadmap for achieving sustainable development that benefits both people and the planet.

When we look at Sustainability, we do not look at the environmental portion only – to me, it's the overall Sustainability of the business, and I find Business Continuity Plan quite close to it. Sustainability and Business Continuity Plan both work towards the long-term viability of the organization. And hence, I find this definition close to my heart - Sustainability refers to the ability of an organization to operate in a way that is environmentally, socially, and economically responsible in the long term. On the other hand, Business Continuity Plan is the process of creating and maintaining a plan that ensures a company can continue to operate during and after a disruptive event.

In the table below, I attempt to show this relationship with a couple of examples:

Sustainability	**Business Continuity Plan**
Energy-efficient practices	Better management of power outages
Waste reduction program	Better management of waste during a disruption – perhaps we all ignored this angle during the Covid-19 Pandemic, where a huge amount of biowaste was generated, and a massive amount of e-waste is going to be ready in the next couple of years when all the new equipment is going to have lived its age.
Waste, environmental damage, and social impacts on the management of the supply chain	Developing a resilient supply chain
Community engagement	Increased resilience by involving communities in BC Program

By investing in sustainability initiatives, a company can attract customers who value environmentally and socially responsible practices. Similarly, by having a robust Business Continuity Plan in place, a company can build resilience and reduce the risk of financial losses due to disruptions, which can help ensure its long-term viability. Both lure customers (external as well as internal).

Business Continuity Planning (Business Continuity Plan) can support several of the United Nations Sustainable Development Goals (SDGs). These goals include:

- **Goal 8:** Decent Work and Economic Growth - Business Continuity Plan can help ensure that organizations are able to continue their operations during and after a disruptive event, which can help maintain employment and contribute to economic growth.
- **Goal 9:** Industry, Innovation, and Infrastructure-Business Continuity Plan can help ensure the continuity of critical infrastructure, such as ICT, Buildings and others.
- **Goal 11:** Sustainable Cities and Communities- Business Continuity Plan can help ensure that essential services continue to be provided in urban areas during and after a disruptive event, such as emergency response services and waste management.
- **Goal 12:** Responsible Consumption and Production- A business Continuity Plan can help minimize waste and reduce the environmental impact of a disruptive event by ensuring that resources are used efficiently and effectively.

- **Goal 13:** Climate Action - Business Continuity Plan can help organizations prepare for the impacts of climate change and reduce their greenhouse gas emissions through measures such as energy-efficient operations and the use of renewable energy sources.

Overall, Business Continuity Plan can play an important role in supporting sustainable development by helping organizations maintain their operations and minimize the impact of disruptive events on people, the environment, and the economy.

Put together, Sustainability and Business Continuity Planning can become a deadly combination – a differentiator for an organization – providing a competitive edge!

A typical Business Continuity Plan Implementation lifecycle contains the following steps (As shown in the diagram above):

1. Manage Program: Policy, Manual
2. Analyse/understand the organization: BIA-RA
3. Design: Strategy
4. Implement: Plans (BC/Incident-Crisis/Emergency/Communication/ITDR/Information-Cybersecurity)
5. Validate: Test, review, Audit
6. Improve Continually
7. Embed: Training/Awareness

The following table shows the key outputs from these lifecycle stages:

S.No.	Lifecycle stage	Key Activities/outputs
1.	Manage Program	BCM Manual (objectives, scope, context, interested parties), Policy
2.	Analyse/Understand the organisation	Business Impact Analysis (BIA), Risk Assessment (RA)
3.	Design	Strategies/solutions
4.	Implement	BCM Plans (emergency, incident/crisis, crisis communication, continuity, IT disaster recovery, cybersecurity etc.)
5.	Validate	Reviews, tests, audits
6.	Improve continually	Plans and arrangements
7.	Embed	Training and awareness for all (appropriate complexity/coverage)

The picture below helps to understand that Business Continuity Plan/BCM (Business Continuity Management) is everyone's business.

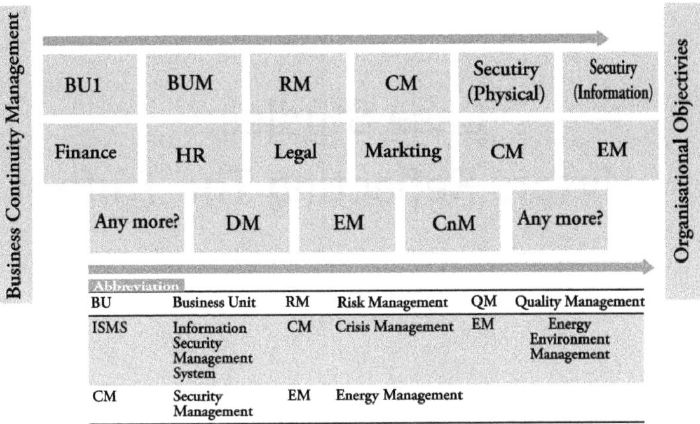

A business Continuity Plan also has linkages with other domains/programs (IT Disaster Recovery being one of those) in an organization. These include:

- ERM
- Crisis Management
- Crisis Communication
- ITDR, Information Security, Cybersecurity
- Health & Safety
- ESG, and Sustainability

The business of business is making money (in an ethical way, of course). The day one thinks of B the business, they must think of B the Business Continuity! And its journey of transformation – to be improved continually.

5

Case Studies: Mirrors Reflecting The Truth

Case Study 1

The Frantic Call

About the company

- 1,100 crores turnover, 20% growth
- 50 years of business presence
- 700 employees with 5 offices across India
- In the Plastic Mould Designing Space

1.15 AM: Ring Ring "What happened, Ramesh? Why are you bothering me at 1.15 AM". "Anand Jee, I am not able to get ERP up, possibly some minor mistake, but bills are required for early morning shipments. We will lose 3 Cr if shipments don't go. Could you please help?"

Anand: "*Kabtak tum Nahin Sikhoge, Remote Do*". [When will you learn, give me the remote.]

Ramesh: "Sir, nothing seems to be working; I will show you through a WhatsApp Video Call, *Kahin Ransomware Attack to Nahin ho Gaya*". [Do you think this could be a Ransomware Attack]

Anand: "Restart the server, don't scare me right in the morning; we have one of the best Security Systems implemented."

Ramesh: "I have done that already. Please accept the Video Call."

Anand: "Let me call our security vendor. They are the best name in the country; I am sure they will make it work."

Next Few Hours, 10 people get to work from across the world, and they find a message demanding $2.8 M USD; it is clear that it is a Ransomware attack!

They did not realize that they were breached 2 weeks back. It started with an endpoint of an operational trainee having design software misbehaving. They did not think too much of it till 2 more endpoints misbehaved, which escalated to the IT Team.

Even then, they did not realize the full extent of the breach. It was when their core ERP System went down that they realized there was an issue. All the data disks got encrypted, and all the VMs & physical servers were down. Their Datacentre went completely offline.

The problems

- **Manual/script-based backup policy in place**
    - ❖ Processes were not followed for daily Backup in view of the unprecedented work pressure of extra billings and new Security layer evaluation.

  - ❖ Data from the last 2 weeks was not backed up.
- **No checklist for early detection & what to do in case of a breach.**
  - ❖ Early warning of endpoint misbehaviour was ignored as it did not reach IT.
  - ❖ And hence they realized it late and then brought their whole network down because of not having any checklist in place.
- **No DR Site**
  - ❖ And hence no replicated data.
- **No endpoint security and advanced network security solutions in place**
  - ❖ Because of this, they had to make their Data center offline completely to safeguard it.

One of the Backup & Recovery organizations was identified and onboarded immediately; this came through the Security partner organization.

The extent of the damage

- Encrypted storage drives of about 30 TB of data would take a lot of time and money to recover since they were not backed up.
- A network that was completely offline, even for SaaS applications access.
- 5-day n night work by the IT team and the right partner to recover their IT setup.
- Loss of 3 full days of business.

- Partial data loss.
- Unmeasurable reputation loss.
- Ramesh showed maturity beyond his years in managing & responding to crises and looked at multiple ways to locate the lost data minimizing the loss.

The Backup partner mitigated future risks and became their partner in setting up a

- Training for the Mindset of critical business and IT person for Data Backup is one of the top priorities.
- Exhaustive Business Continuity Plan from the Backup prospective process, due to which the business suffered
- Outsourcing Backup, one DGM Single point of contact, and one IT person scheduled for giving 15 mins each day for vendor interactions.
- One Offline copy of the entire Data
- Qtrly audit of processes being followed

Security Partner worked in partnership with the Backup partner and also set up an exhaustive system for endpoint security, quarterly audit of security & processes in case of a breach.

CIO Anand could stand in front of management in 3 months' time and say that from now onwards; they are ready for any eventuality through Data Recovery with a max RPO of 2 hrs and an RTO of zero to 24 hrs for various applications.

CIO Anand and Ramesh got a major raise in their salaries 6 months down the line.

Case Study 2

AIIMS Data Breach (Successful near complete data restoration)

In Nov 2022, a major incident shook the entire IT & medical fraternity.

Key highlights

- 1.3 TB data on possibly 5 of 100+ servers was corrupted.
- CERT-IN was involved.
- Backed-up data was used, and all data was recovered.
- The whole service was manual for almost a week.
- The patient records of multiple lakhs of patients, including VIPs & VVIPs, were restored.
- Imagine what would have happened to the country's reputation and critical data if proper Backup would not have been in place.

Learnings

A. Backup Mindset is critical for all kinds of organizations.

B. Backup Rule Book creation, implementation and review are critical

C. No organization is safe from Cyber Attacks.

D. Rigorous work is required on Data Backup.

Cyber security incident at AIIMS | National Informatics Centre team working at AIIMS suspects it to be a ransomware attack. As of 7:30 pm hospital services are running on manual mode: AIIMS

7:48 PM · Nov 23, 2022

75 Retweets **9** Quotes **582** Likes **6** Bookmarks

6

Backup Vs Back Up, The Evolution of Backup & Related Storage: Fun Facts

We have been talking about the criticality and importance of data and the challenges in implementing it throughout this book. Now let's take a look at some other interesting aspects of Backup.

BACKUP Vs BACK UP: FUN FACTS

All that separates the spelling of these words is a single space. The **verb** form, referring to the process of doing so, is "**Back up**", whereas the **noun** and adjective form is "**Backup**".

Backup (Noun and Adjective)

"a standby, a reserve"

This word originated in the second half of the 1700s. It was originally used for armed forces, police or singers, backup army, backup police team/officer, and backup singer

http://www.enhancemywriting.com/backup-vs-back-up

A specific reference to computing is from 1965

https://www.etymonline.com/word/backup

It is an extra or secondary version of something, but now in IT/Computer Lingo, it is used as "Backup or data backup is a copy of computer data taken and stored elsewhere so that it may be used to restore the original after a data loss event.

Backup could also be used as "Backup" when used as an adjective.

Back-up is a verb phrase,

To move backwards, to 1767, "stand behind and support," from **back** (v.) + **up** (adv.). The meaning "move or force backward" is by 1834. Of water prevented from flowing by 1837.

https://www.etymonline.com/word/back%20 up?ref=etymonline_crossreference#etymonline_v_26820

Back

Mid-15c., "to keep something back, hinder," from back (adv.). The meaning "cause to move back" is from 1781. The intransitive sense of "move or go back" is from late 15c. The meaning "furnish with a back or backing" is from 1728, from back (n.). The meaning "to support" (as by a bet) is attested from the 1540s. Related: Backed; backing.

up (adv.)

up

Old English up, uppe, from Proto-Germanic *upp- "up" (source also of Old Frisian, Old Saxon up "up, upward," Old Norse upp; Danish, Dutch op; Old High German uf, German auf "up"; Gothic iup "up, upward," uf "on, upon, under;" Old High German oba, German ob "over, above, on, upon"), from PIE root *upo "under," also "up from under," hence also "over."

As a preposition, "to a higher place" from c. 1500; also "along, through" (1510s), "toward" (1590s). Often used elliptically for go up, come up, rise up, etc. **Up the river** "in jail" first recorded 1891, originally in reference to Sing Sing, which is up the Hudson from New York City. To drive someone **up the wall** (1951) is from the notion of the behavior of lunatics or caged animals. Insulting retort **up yours** (scil. ass) is attested by late 19c.

Accumulate too much, to support, or to reinforce Back up did not have a definition of duplicate copy of something till second mid of 1900s, support someone or something in Auxiliary way, to create a copy of something for use in case of Disaster.

Evolution of Backup and Some Storage Types

Backup, as done in current times, came into being possibly in the mid-1970s and would continue to evolve as more and more Zetta Bytes of data keep getting added and becoming critical for states, Organizations, societies, homes and individuals.

The timelines given below are to give a broad idea and not to be quoted as exhaustively researched; these are based on the knowledge of the author over the years:

1775: Punch Card

1846: Punch Tape

1940s: Magnetic Drums used by US Navy for Backup

1951: Magnetic Tape

1952: Tape Drive

1956: Magnetic Hard drive

1960s: Mag disks for Backup

1963: RAM was patented

1971: 1st Floppy Drive sold by IBM

1972: Cassette launched

Mid-1970s: Sunguard info system, for its internal systems, made back up solution.

1978: 1st Customer in open space by Sunguard, info systems, 1st backup hot site

1979-80: Desktop backup became a thing

1980: Flash Drive/Pen Drive

1984: DEC's Mag tape, later called DLT

1985: Computer-readable CD-ROM

1989: IBM entered the backup market

1989: NAS came to market

1989: CDP patented

1989: HP data protector through Apollo acquisition

1990: Networker launched as Legato

1990: Arcserve launched

1991: Atempo SA Formed, SSD launched.

1990s: Data Base Online Backup

Mid 1990s: Cloud Backup

1996: Commvault Founded

1997: SAN Launched

1997: Veritas came to Backup

1998: iSCSI enabling Block Storage

2000: LTO-1 by IBM, HP, Seagate

2000: Virtualization start

2003: Acronics Founded

2004: De-duplication in Backup

2006: AWS 1st Cloud Storage

2006: MSP models

2006: Carbonite & Veeam founded

2007: DLT manufacturing stopped by Quantum

2007: Datto Inc & Mozy Founded

2008: Few unstructured data Backup solutions launched

2008: Druva Founded, HAMR developed

2008-9: Data De-duplication in Backup

2009: Alaro, Actifio & Zerto

2010: LTO-5 Launched

2011: NVMe Launched

2012: Parablu Founded

2012: LTO-6 launched

2013: Cohesity Founding year

2015: LTO-7 launched

2017: LTO-8:launched

2021: LTO-9 Launched

2022: Multi-cloud becoming localized

2023: AI/ML innovations drive in Backup/Storage

7

Conclusion

There are multiple other Critical Data Management aspects for Backup, such as:

- DR sites & their automation.
- Multiple complex heterogeneous scenarios, containerization, and multiple virtual mixes.
- Multi-cloud, cloud integration, cloud migration, reverse cloud.
- Data Visibility.
- One Drive, Google Drive, are they really Backup or largely unmanaged data copy, archival. We touched upon this one earlier in the 7th habit, but we would love to cover more on this.
- Smart city backup
- Archival of data

And others which we could not pen down, they would be a lot of matter for another book.

Even the 9 habits given above have been touched upon briefly in view of the limitations of space and time. Archival of Data for unstructured and structured data has also been touched upon briefly only. That too, is content for a complete book specifically for unstructured data, which should be next one.

However, this book is written with the intent of helping you make a paradigm shift in this critical aspect of data Backup that impacts each and every organization, even though the impact may not be directly visible.

So is the case with Family; there is no end to the number of pages that could be dedicated to this most crucial part of our lives. Here I have intended a paradigm shift in how we view, treat and interact with our family, our Backup & Support System in Life.

I would be happy to be reached at **kamal.gulati@itsimple.in** for a mutually convenient timeline to further discuss and contribute to your Backup issues.

In our journey to create awareness about the criticality of data Backup, we are also putting up more and more relevant material on our website www.itsimple.in/MrBackup2 for details of different aspects of Backup discussed in the book. Please do visit the same and check.

I also take this opportunity to remind and invite each one of you to have your organization implement the data Backup habits to the tee, as per the guidelines given in this book or customized/expanded as per your organization's requirement.

Please go ahead and explore this age-old yet not worked upon in detail habit (Backup) by a majority of the organizations.

It Could Possibly be a Matter of Life
and Death for Your Organization.

www.ingramcontent.com/pod-product-compliance
Ingram Content Group UK Ltd.
Pitfield, Milton Keynes, MK11 3LW, UK
UKHW021656190726
13853UKWH00001B/302

9 789355 545350